THE PASTON
MEDIEVAL L...

HISTORY EYEWITNESS

EDITED WITH AN INTRODUCTION
AND ADDITIONAL MATERIAL BY
MARTYN WHITTOCK

HEINEMANN

Published by Heinemann Library,
an imprint of Heinemann Publishers (Oxford) Ltd,
Halley Court, Jordan Hill, Oxford OX2 8EJ

OXFORD LONDON EDINBURGH MADRID
ATHENS BOLOGNA PARIS MELBOURNE
SYDNEY AUCKLAND SINGAPORE TOKYO
IBADAN NAIROBI HARARE GABORONE
PORTSMOUTH NH (USA)

99 98 97 96 95
10 9 8 7 6 5 4 3 2 1

British Library Cataloguing in Publication Data is available
from the British Library on request.

ISBN 0 431 07159 4

Designed by Saffron House, map by Jeff Edwards
Printed and bound in China

Acknowledgements
The publishers would like to thank the following for
permission to reproduce photographs:

His Grace the Archbishop of Canterbury and the Trustees of
Lambeth Palace Library: p.21
Giraudon/Musée Condé, Chantilly: p.11
King's College, Cambridge: p.4
All other photographs, including the cover, courtesy of the
British Library.

Every effort has been made to contact copyright holders of material
reproduced in this book. Any omissions will be rectified in
subsequent printings if notice is given to the publisher.

This book is dedicated to my brothers Paul and Chris.

Note to the reader

In this book some of the words are printed in **bold** type. This indicates that the
word is listed in the glossary on pages 46–7. The glossary gives a brief explanation
of words that may be new to you.

CONTENTS

Introduction

The Paston Letters give us an amazing glimpse into the lives of men and women living in the 15th century and the early part of the 16th century. They show us something of what life was like at the end of the period that historians call the **Middle Ages**, or **Medieval period** of history. The Pastons came from the county of Norfolk in East Anglia. Members of the family were landowners, soldiers, lawyers, members of parliament, students and members of the royal court. The very first member of the family that we know anything about was Clement Paston, who died in 1419. He lived in the village of Paston, seventeen miles north-east of Norwich. During the 15th century the Pastons became important landowners in Norfolk. They made friends as well as enemies and the letters tell us about some of the violent conflicts they had with powerful neighbours who challenged the Paston's rights to own important land, or **manors**.

The collection of letters began in the lifetime of William Paston I (1378–1444) – Clement's son – when Henry VI was King of England. The last letter in the collection dates from around 1506 when Henry VII was King. There are about 1000 letters in the final collection of letters and documents, most of which date from between 1425 and 1499. They cover the period of time in which England experienced the **Wars of the Roses**, and the beginning of **Tudor** rule.

All wealthy families would have written letters like those kept by the Pastons. What is so surprising about them is how many of them have survived. The first writers kept the letters that they received and often kept copies of those letters that were sent to people who were not members of the family. Over time a great collection of documents grew up. This archive was stored in boxes at Oxnead, which by the 18th century had become the main Paston home. In 1732 William Paston, Earl of Yarmouth, died and the collection was broken up.

During the 18th century, collectors bought some of the letters. The first definite mention of them is in 1782. People became interested in trying to trace what had happened to the rest. Some of the letters were published in 1787 and 1789. More were published in 1823 and a man named J. Gairdner brought together collections published in 1875, 1896, 1901 and a six-volume collection in 1904.

Six collections of the main surviving letters were bought by the British Museum between 1866 and 1933. Some of the other letters are now kept in the Bodleian Library and Magdalen College in Oxford. Five of the letters were bought by Pembroke College in Cambridge. Ten letters and documents are in the Pierpont Morgan Library in New York.

The people who wrote them had no idea that their letters and other documents would one day be on public display. They were written as private, personal letters to their family, friends and important servants.

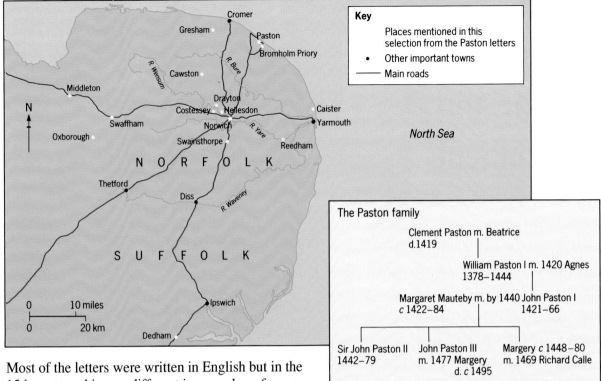

The following is a map of Norfolk and Suffolk with the key and the Paston family tree.

Key

Places mentioned in this selection from the Paston letters

• Other important towns

— Main roads

The Paston family

Clement Paston m. Beatrice
d.1419

William Paston I m. 1420 Agnes
1378–1444

Margaret Mauteby m. by 1440 John Paston I
c 1422–84 1421–66

Sir John Paston II
1442–79

John Paston III
m. 1477 Margery
d. c 1495

Margery c 1448–80
m. 1469 Richard Calle

Members of the Paston family mentioned in this selection of letters.

Most of the letters were written in English but in the 15th century this was different in a number of ways from modern English. Here is how Agnes Paston wrote to her husband asking him to buy some clothes for the girl they were planning for their son to marry:

> 'Dere housband, I recomaunde me to yow. Blessyd be God and I sende yow gode tydyngs of the gentylwomman that ye wetyn of. Yif ye wolde byin her a goune, here moder wolde yeve ther to a godely furre. The goune nedyth for to be had; and of a colour it wolde be a godely blew...'

The spelling of some words is different from modern English. Many words are no longer used. In modern English the letter reads:

> 'Dear husband, I recommend myself to you. Blessed be God and I send you good news about the gentlewoman that you know about. If you would buy her a gown (dress) her mother will get a fur for it. The gown needs to be bought and the best colour for it would be blue...'

In this collection all of the letters have been turned into modern English to make it easier for you to read them. Only a tiny selection of the huge number of letters in the collection has been chosen, in order to give you a glimpse into the life of the Paston family. The letters have been grouped together in themes, so as to give information about different aspects of life.

War and Government

The letters in this Chapter some of which are from good friends of the Pastons deal with politics and warfare. The first tells of a sea battle against the French (Letter 1). Letter 2 is concerned with stopping powerful neighbours from treating weaker people badly. Letter 3 contains information about the King – Henry VI – who was mentally ill – and about news of powerful people at court competing for power. There are reports of a battle – the Battle of St Albans (Letter 4). At the Battle of Barnet (Letter 5), Sir John Paston and his brother fought on the losing side and were captured by the army of Edward of York. All of these battles were fought in the English Wars of the Roses. A letter sent home from Calais keeps the family informed about the war being fought between England and France (Letter 6).

LETTER 1

Robert Wenyngton to Thomas Daniel.
25 May, 1449.

Most reverend master,

I recommend myself to your gracious mastership. First I shall send you word that when we went to sea we captured two ships from Brest [in Brittany, France]. Then we met with a fleet of 100 great ships and I commanded them to surrender in the name of the King of England. Then I told them that unless they surrendered, I would **oversail** them. And they told me to do my worst, because I had so few ships that they did not fear me. But as God willed, on Friday last, we had a good wind and we armed 2000 men in all my ships and made ready to oversail them. Then they launched a boat and put up a flag of truce and came and spoke with me. And they surrendered all their ships to go with me to the place I commanded. But they had fought with me the day before and shot at us 1000 guns and **quarrels** beyond number, and killed many in my fellow ships. Therefore I decided that they should lose all their ships as our sovereign lord the King commands. And so I have brought these ships to the Isle of Wight.

You should get permission from our sovereign lord the King to come here, for you never saw so many ships taken into England this winter. We are armed night and day to keep them until we have news from our sovereign and his **council**. And so come here yourself and you will have great honour to see such a sight. For I have at this time captured all the chief ships of Holland, Zealand and Flanders.

I write no more to you at this time but Almighty Jesus take care of you. I write this in haste on the Isle of Wight, on Sunday, the night after the **Ascension of Our Lord**.

The Battle of Sluys from a 15th century manuscript. During the 15th century soldiers were as important as sailors in sea battles. Each end of the ship had a castle and the fighting was mainly done by men armed as if they were on land. In the ship on the left you can see both longbowmen and crossbowmen.

LETTER 2

Sir John Fastolf to Thomas Howys, his friend.
20 December, 1450.

Right trusty friend,

I greet you well. Such people who have found they are troubled by **extortion**, just like I have been, must make this known to my Lord Oxford and to my brother so that they will make sure that justice is given out equally. They must not deny their support for poor people, otherwise the poor people and the largest part of Norfolk and Suffolk will be destroyed. For it is clear that the poor have lived in misery and poverty for many years. Most poor people have little or nothing to keep themselves alive, or pay the King's taxes, or their rents and **service** to their lords, and this is shown daily to the world which is a great pity.

I understand, by a letter sent to me from my well loved friend Master John Botewryght, that great extortions have been carried out by the officers of the Duke of Suffolk by stealing many acres of pasture at Swaffham which belong to the King and are part of his land as Duke of Lancaster. And if these pastures are not returned, it will be a great

The meeting of the men of Essex and the men of Kent during the Peasants' Revolt, from a 15th century manuscript. The peasants have been painted as men at arms rather than as peasants. They have the armour and equipment of 15th century foot soldiers.

loss to the king and to the **tenants** there and because of this, Master John [Botewryght] asks for help in the name of all the people of Swaffham.

All those who have been badly treated should – according to the advice given by well educated men – put their sufferings and complaints in writing, with evidence, and explain the truth of the situation. Then the writing or **bill** must be sealed with the **seals** of those gentlemen who live there and those men who are well known. And that writing should be sent to the King and to the lords of his council. And this will be more likely to be believed than a simple letter. And if these complaints are shown here to the King and the lords, it is fair to think that they will get the matter sorted out.

LETTER 3

John Stodeley to the Duke of Norfolk.
19 January, 1454.

Regarding news, may it please you to know that when the Prince [Edward] came to Windsor the Duke of Buckingham took him in his arms and showed him to the King pleading with him to bless him, but the King did not answer him. Despite this the duke stayed with the Prince and the King and when he could get no answer the Queen came in and took the Prince in her arms and showed him, like the duke had done, but it was no good and they left without getting any answer [from the King] except that he looked at the Prince and cast his eyes down.

Also the cardinal has commanded all his servants to be ready with bows and arrows, swords and shields, crossbows and all other weapons of war that they can get hold of and be ready to protect him.

Also the Earl of Wiltshire and the Lord Bonvile have commanded that it be announced at Taunton in Somersetshire that every man that is able and ready should go with them and serve them and be paid 6 **pence** a day.

Also the Duke of Exeter himself has been to Tuxforth near Doncaster, in the north of the country, and there Lord Egremont met him and these two promised help for each other and the duke has come back home again.

Also a letter has gone to the lords requesting to have a **garrison** at Windsor to protect the King and the Prince and that they should have money to pay their wages.

Also the Queen has put together a list with five requests and the first of these is that she wants to rule this land. The second is that she should decide who will be **Chancellor**, the **Treasurer**, the **Privy Seal** and all other officials in this land along with **sheriffs** and all the other officials that the King should decide about. The third is that she should control all the bishops in the land. The fourth is that she should have enough money given her to look after the King, the Prince and herself. But as for the fifth article – I do not know what it is.

LETTER 4

John Crane to John Paston.
25 May, 1455.

To my worshipful and well loved cousin John Paston.

This letter is delivered in haste. This is the news we have here – these lords are dead: the Duke of Somerset, the Earl of Northumberland and the Lord Clyfford. As for any other lords, many of them are hurt.

And as to whether a great number of people were killed, there were at the most six **score.** And as for the lords who were with the King, they have been pillaged and robbed of all their harness and horses. As for who will rule us now, I do not know except certain new officials have been appointed.

My lord [Duke] of York has been made **Constable of England**; my lord [Earl] of Warwick has been made **Captain of Calais**; my Lord Burgchier has been made Treasurer. I have not got any other news.

And as for our sovereign lord, thank God he has not been hurt very much.

No more [news] to you at this time but I ask you send this letter to my Mistress Paston when you have seen it. Please think of my sister Margaret at that time when she becomes a nun. Written on **Whitsunday**.

LETTER 5

Sir John Paston II to his mother Margaret Paston.
18 April, 1471.

Mother,

God be blessed, my brother is alive and keeping well and is in no danger of being killed. Nevertheless he has been hurt with an arrow on his right arm below the elbow and I have sent him a surgeon who has dressed the wound. He tells me that he is sure that he will be well in a very short time.

BATTLE OF ST ALBANS, 1455

This was the first battle in the Wars of the Roses. In 1454, Henry VI recovered from his first attack of madness. Richard Duke of York, who had governed the country while the King was ill, was removed from power by Queen Margaret – Henry's wife – and her friend the Duke of Somerset. Richard fought back and won the Battle of St Albans, which was fought on 22 May, 1455. The battle only lasted for just over one hour. The King's army was in St Albans trying to block the route to London. Most of the fighting took place in St Peter's Street in the town. One of the powerful men killed in the battle was the Duke of Somerset. He was one of the friends of the Queen and a supporter of the King. This battle put King Henry back under the control of Richard, Duke of York.

Kings and knights praying, from an illustration in a 15th century prayer book. Many great nobles had beautiful prayer books, with the text copied out by hand and illustrations painted by specialist artists.

These are the people killed on the battlefield, half a mile from Barnet, on Easter Day. The Earl of Warwick, the Marquis Montagu, Sir William Tyrell and many other **esquires** of this country.

As for other news – Queen Margaret and her son have landed in the West Country and I believe that tomorrow, or the next day, King Edward will leave here and drive her out again.

Written at London the Thursday in Easter week. I hope soon to see you. Keep this letter secret. If you do nothing to make my enemies suspect you I am sure all will be well. If things go on as they are, I will be alright as will the rest of us.

Henry VI and his parliament from a 15th century manuscript. The picture shows the ideas that people at the time had about power – it passes from God to the King to the members of the House of Lords and then to the members of the House of Commons.

LETTER 6

*Edward Benyngfield to Sir John Paston II.
17 August, 1477.*

Master Paston,

As for news from these parts, the French King is laying **siege** to St Omer [a town in the English-held region around Calais] on one side of the town, and people from the town **skirmish** with them [the French] every day. The French King has burned all the towns and abbeys that were around St Omer, and also the corn which was growing there.

And I understand that the emperor's son has been married at Ghent [in Flanders] and brought with him only 400 horsemen 100,000 **ducats**, which is not enough for what he needs to do [help the English fight the French] and so I am afraid that Flanders will be lost [to the French].

The 15th century was very violent and the Paston letters tell us a lot about violent disagreements between the Pastons and various neighbours. The Pastons were forced to ask the King to help them get back a manor stolen from them by a rival (Letters 1 and 5) and they were continually attempting to get Royal support by sending formal requests in the form of petitions. Margaret Paston's shopping list at the time, sent to her husband in London, included crossbows as well as almonds and sugar (Letter 2).

Some of these disagreements were over small matters. The Pastons extended one of their boundary walls and blocked part of a nearby road. This led to violent reactions from their neighbours (Letters 3 and 4). Other disagreements were more serious. Every effort was made to try to get help from the King (Letter 5) while enemies used violence against the family.

Animals taken from a man trespassing on Paston land led to a bitter battle with the Duke of Suffolk and his men (Letters 6, 7, and 8) in which even the church was not safe (Letter 9).

CHAPTER 2

Problems with the Neighbours

LETTER 1

A petition from John Paston to Parliament.
Summer 1449.

To the King our sovereign lord, and to the wise lords brought together in this Parliament.

Your humble servant begs that he has peacefully owned the manor of Gresham, in the county of Norfolk, for more than 20 years, until the 17th day of February [1448], when Lord Moleyns entered that manor. I asked Lord Moleyns politely to leave daily, from the time he entered until the next Feast of **Michaelmas** [29th, September, 1448]. On 6th October I was forced to move into another house, until 28th January [1449] when Lord Moleyns sent there a violent group of people to the number of a thousand. They were armed with cuirasses, **briganders** and **jacks**, **sallets**, spears, bows, guns, long hooks to pull down houses, and battering rams with which they broke down the gates and doors and got into the house. Inside was my wife and twelve other people. These twelve people were driven out of the house and the wall of the room which my wife was in, was broken down and she was taken out. They cut apart the pillars of the house and let them fall and broke up all the rooms and carried off all the stuff to the value of £200. And still these criminals, against the law, hold on to the manor using force and lie in wait for my friends, tenants and servants.

LETTER 2

Margaret Paston to her husband John Paston.
Probably 1449.

Right worshipful husband,

I recommend myself to you and ask you to get some crossbows and **wyndlacs** to wind them with and quarrels. For this house has so few of them that none of our men can shoot out, although we have never had so much need.

Partryche [one of Lord Moleyn's men] and his friends are frightened that you will get in [to the house they had taken from the Pastons]. They have made bars to bar the doors, and they have made **wykets** on every corner of the house to shoot out through, both with bows and hand-guns.

A boy in a fruit tree, from a marginal illustration in a 15th century manuscript. Scribes often livened up their manuscripts by painting funny pictures in the margins. In this case the boy has been caught taking fruit.

I ask that you will make sure that you buy me 1lb of almonds and sugar and that you will buy some **frese** to make a gown for your child. And would you buy a yard of black broadcloth for a hood for me, for there is neither good cloth, nor good frese, in this town. And when I have them, I will make the child his gown.

LETTER 3

Agnes Paston to her son John Paston.
1451.

To Barker of St Mary Clement's parish, in Norwich, to deliver to Master John Paston in haste.

On Thursday the servants built the wall a yard high, and a good while before evening there was heavy rain. The servants were forced to leave the work. There has been so much water that it stands a foot deep under the wall towards Ball's land [a neighbour]. And on Friday after **mass**, someone came from church and pushed down all that was built there and trod on the wall and broke some – but I cannot discover who did it. And Warne Kynge's wife cursed Ball [a neighbour of Pastons] as she crossed the stile and said that he had given away the path and made it John Paston's private land.

Yesterday evening, when I was going to my bed, the vicar said that Warne Kynge and Warne Harman took Sir Robert [the curate] in the **vestry** and told him to tell me that the wall will be pulled down again.

LETTER 4

Agnes Paston to her son John Paston.
November 1451.

I spoke this day with a man from Paston [the village] and he told me that another man told him that men from Paston would not go on procession further than the churchyard on St Mark's day. For the route of the procession was blocked, and that men hoped that in a short time the wall would be broken down again. He said that I was fined for blocking the road at the last court but he could not tell me how much the fine was!

LETTER 5

Sir John Paston II to his father John Paston.
23 August, 1461.

Most reverend and worshipful father,

I recommend myself heartily and submit myself humbly to your fatherhood, asking you for help. I beg you to excuse me for not writing. I have daily tried to get my Lord of Essex to persuade the King to do something about the manor of Dedham and I have often asked him if he has persuaded the King regarding this. He answered

LAW AND ORDER

It was very difficult to keep law and order in the 15th century. There was no police force and it was very hard to prove that a person was guilty of a crime. Crime seems to have increased in the 1450s and 1460s when the King was not fully in control of the country. If a person was accused of a crime they would be tried by a 'jury', made up of local people. Often these juries were bribed or threatened to make sure that a guilty person went unpunished. Many people who were guilty of violent crimes were pardoned by the King. Often this was in return for going to fight in the King's army.

me 'no', saying it was not the time and said he would like to hurry it along as much as I did. Often I felt so delayed that I thought to tell you that I feared he was not willing to persuade the King. Nevertheless I worked on him continually.

And now, recently, I reminded him of the same matter and enquired if he had influenced the King's highness and he answered me that he had spoken to the King concerning this matter of the manor of Dedham, begging him to be your good lord, remembering the good service you have done. The King said he would be your good lord as he would be to the poorest man in England. He would support your rights but as for showing you favour, he would not be thought of as showing favouritism to one man more than another.

I suppose you understand that the money that I had from you at London may not last me until the King goes to Wales and comes home again, for I understand that it will be long before he comes home again. Because of this, I have sent to London, to my Uncle Clement, to get 100 **shillings**. I beg you not to be displeased with me for I could not make any other arrangement, unless I had borrowed it from a stranger, which I think you would not have liked if you had heard about it later.

There is talk here how you and Howard fought together on the **shireday** and one of Howard's men struck you twice with a dagger and you should have been hurt but for a good **doublet** that you had on at the time. Blessed be God that you had it on. I write no more to your good fatherhood at this time, but Almighty God have you in His keeping and send you victory over your enemies.

LETTER 6

Margaret Paston to her husband John Paston.
10 May, 1465.

Piers Waryn ploughed up your land at Drayton and so your servants took the mares from his plough to stop him and brought them to Hellesdon [a manor owned by the Pastons] and there they are still. The next morning, Master Philip and the bailiff of Costessey [the Duke of Suffolk's men] came to Hellesdon with a great number of people and took from the parson's plough two horses (worth 4 **marks**), and two horses from Thomas Stermyn's plough (worth 40 shillings). They said that they were taken because of a claim against them in the **Hundred Court**, brought by Piers, because his plough horses had been taken.

Left. A mid-15th century law court, from a contemporary manuscript. Keeping written records was an important part of a court's function. During peasants' revolts court records were often the first things the peasants captured and destroyed. The records listed all the duties they owed to the local landowners.

THE SERVANTS OF POWERFUL LANDOWNERS

By the 15th century many powerful landowners kept and paid for a large number of servants. These people were loyal to their lord, or lady, in return for pay, or a 'fee', and often clothing, or 'livery'. They often wore particular colours, or badges, to show whose servant they were. These servants often made up a private army for rich people. It was very difficult to stand up to such powerful landowners and most people tried to make sure that they were on the right side of their local lord. It was very dangerous to fall out with such a lord or his friends and servants. Those who did so were often violently attacked.

TRAVEL

The Paston family spent a lot of their time travelling. They moved between their different manors in Norfolk during the year, regardless of the weather and the state of the roads. Leading members of the family went to London to the royal court and the law courts, leaving their families behind to battle with their neighbours. Others were with English soldiers at Calais trying to defend what remained of English territory in France, and negotiate with enemies of the French in Flanders.

The same afternoon the parson of Hellesdon sent his men to speak to Master Philip to find out if there was any way of getting the animals back. Master Philip answered that if they would repay Piers Waryn for his trouble then he would give them back; otherwise he would not. And Master Philip said openly that if any of your servants made any trouble, even if it cost him a chicken, they would come and take back the price of an ox! And if they could not find something worth that, they would break into your tenants' houses in Hellesdon and take as much as they could find inside. And if they are stopped from doing this, then they will go into any of your property in Norfolk and Suffolk and cause trouble there!

Richard Calle [a faithful Paston servant] asked the parson and Stermyn if they would take any action to get back their animals. The parson said that he was old and sick and he did not want any trouble. He said he would rather lose his cattle, for if he took any action they would cause him so much trouble that he would never be free from them.

Skipwith [a friendly neighbour] went with me to the Bishop of Norwich and I told him about the riotous and evil behaviour of Master Philip. He said to me that he owed you goodwill and wished that you were at home. He said to me that it would be a great comfort to your friends and neighbours and that your presence would do more good that a hundred of your men could with you away.

LETTER 7

Margaret Paston to her husband John Paston.
12 July, 1465.

The Duke of Suffolk's men daily threaten Richard Calle [and other servants] that wherever they find them they will kill them. Attacks have been made on Richard Calle this week, so that he was in great danger at Norwich. And great attacks have been made on me and my people here last Monday. Richard Calle tells me that he has written to you about it more plainly than I do at this time, but I will let you know more later.

I suppose there will be trouble against your servants at the **assize** and it would seem a good idea if you would speak with the **justices** before they come here. I will do as you advise me to do, for what with sickness and trouble that I have had, I have been brought very low and weak but I will do the best I can for you.

LETTER 8

Margaret Paston to her husband John Paston.
17 October, 1465.

The Duke of Suffolk came to Norwich on Tuesday, with about 500 men. He sent for the mayor and **aldermen**, asking them in the King's name to find out from the **constables** of every **ward** in the city, the names of any men who had gone to help your men at any time. If they find them, they should arrest them and punish them and give him their names.

The lodge and all that remains of your place was broken down on Tuesday and Wednesday. And this night, at midnight, a group of men brought a cart and took away featherbeds and all our stuff that was left at the parson's. Please send me a message telling me what to do. Should I stay at Caister, or come to you at London?

LETTER 9

Margaret Paston to her son, Sir John Paston II.
12 September, 1469.

I greet you well, letting you know that your brother and his people are in great danger at Caister Castle and lack food. Daubeney and Berney [friends of the Pastons] are dead and many others badly hurt. They lack gunpowder and arrows and the place has been badly broken by the guns of our enemies, so that if they do not quickly have help they are likely to lose both their lives and the place. Every man in the country [Norfolk] is astonished that you have allowed them to be in such danger for so long without help, or assistance.

The Duke of Norfolk has been more cruel than before and he has sent for his tenants from every place to be there at Caister on Thursday next. Then there will be the greatest number that there has been there and they intend to make a great attack, for they have sent to Lynn [King's Lynn] for guns. With all their guns it will be impossible for those inside to hold out against them without God's help, or speedy assistance from you.

Peasants being attacked by soldiers or robbers, from a 15th century manuscript. It was easy for fighting men, whether they were part of an official army or not, to take whatever they wanted from peasants. In times of war there could be many bands of soldiers, or ex-soldiers, wandering in the countryside.

CHAPTER 3

Love and Marriage

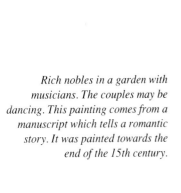

Rich nobles in a garden with musicians. The couples may be dancing. This painting comes from a manuscript which tells a romantic story. It was painted towards the end of the 15th century.

The Paston Letters contain a number of very private letters written between husbands and wives and between lovers. Marriage for those as wealthy as the Pastons was arranged between families and it was a pleasant surprise when the young people, about to get married, got on together (Letter 1).

Marriage was often treated like a business arrangement in which deals had to be agreed (Letter 6). The arrangements for the marriage of daughters would often include the promise of a sum of money, or dowry (Letter 7). However, there could be problems when a family could not raise as much money as the other family demanded. (Letter 8) Any marriage – especially a royal one – was a very important social occasion.

Despite arranged marriages, there could be real love felt between wives and husbands. Margaret Paston was desperately worried when her husband was seriously ill and away from home (Letter 2). Family opposition could make it very hard for two people to marry (Letter 3). This was particularly so when a family felt that the girl had fallen in love with a man who was not as wealthy as the one they had planned for her to marry. Margery Paston fell in love with Richard Calle, a family servant. They promised to marry each other but the family opposed them and tried to keep them apart, causing them great unhappiness (Letter 4). The family even went as far as trying to prove that the promise could be ignored (Letter 5). They failed because the two lovers stuck by their promise – despite the threats. Margery and Richard eventually married, but Margery was disowned by her furious family.

LETTER 1

Agnes Paston to her husband William Paston.
1440.

Dear husband,

I recommend myself to you. Blessed be God, I send you good news about the arrival of the gentlewoman, that you know about, from Reedham.

And as for the first time that John [their son] met this gentlewoman, she gave him a warm welcome. And so I hope there will be no need to arrange things between them.

The parson of Stockton told me that if you will buy this gentlewoman a gown, her mother will get a fur for it. The gown needs to be bought and the best colour for it would be blue or perhaps a bright red.

Please buy me two reels of gold thread. Your fishponds are doing well.

The Holy **Trinity** look after you. Written at Paston in haste, the Wednesday after the third Sunday after Easter, for lack of a good secretary.

LETTER 2

Margaret Paston to her husband John Paston.
28 September, 1443.

Right worshipful husband,

I recommend myself to you, very much longing to hear how you are, thanking God for your recovery from the great illness that you had. And I thank you for the letter that you sent me, for in truth my mother and I were not happy from the time that we heard of your sickness, until we were sure that you were better. My mother promised another image of wax – as heavy as you are! – to **Our Lady of Walsingham.**

Many people in the Middle Ages thought it was very important to go on a pilgrimage. This was a journey to a place which was thought to be very holy. They believed that if they did this then they were more likely to have their prayers answered. Many people came to the village of Walsingham in East Anglia. They believed that the Virgin Mary had made this place very holy and every year it attracted hundreds of pilgrims.

And she sent four nobles to the **friars** at Norwich to pray for you. And I have promised to go on a pilgrimage, for you, to Walsingham. In truth I have never had so worrying a time, from the time that I found out about your sickness until I heard you were better. Still my heart is not happy, nor will it be until I know that you are really better.

I ask you sincerely that you will send me a letter as quick as you can, if writing is no problem for you, and that you will promise to tell me what your sore is like. I would rather have you at home now – if it would make you better, and if your sore could be as well treated here as where you are – than have a gown, even if it were scarlet! I ask you, if your sore is better, and you are able to ride, then when my father comes to London you may ask permission to come home when his horse will be sent home again. For I hope that you will be as well looked after here as you are in London.

LETTER 3

Margaret Paston to her husband John Paston.
29 January, 1454.

Right worshipful husband,

I recommend myself to you. I spoke to my sister yesterday and she told me that she was sorry that she was not able to speak with you before you left. And she asked that you should give 'the gentleman' that you know about such a message that he might feel that you are in favour of 'that matter' that you know about [a marriage]. For she told me that he has said that he thought you did not care much about it. Because of this she asks that you will be her good brother and that you might have a complete answer for her now – whether it is 'yes', or 'no'. For her mother has said to her, since you left, that she is not in favour of it and it will come to nothing. And her mother has said to her that it is wise to delay and spoken to her in a way that she thinks is very strange. And she is tired of it and she desires instead to have it fully sorted out. She says that she fully trusts you and she will agree with whatever you do.

We have no other news. The blissful Trinity have you in his keeping. Written at Norwich, on the Tuesday before **Candlemas**.

I ask that you will make sure to buy a thing for my neck [a necklace].

The month of April from 'The Très Riches Heures' of John, Duke of Berry. This painting shows the extravagant dress of rich European nobles (see page 38). The manuscript book was painted by three brothers called Limbourg, who all died from the plague in 1416. The last page they painted in the book showed a procession in Rome asking God to spare people from a plague.

LETTER 4

Richard Calle, a Paston servant, to Margery Paston,
the lady he promised to marry.
1469.

My own lady and mistress and before God my very true wife.

With my heart full of sorrow, I recommend myself to you as one who cannot be happy. For this life that we are leading is neither pleasing to God nor the world, considering the union of marriage that is made between us and also the great love that has been – and I hope still is – between us. For we who should be together are apart. To me it seems it is a thousand years ago that I spoke to you. I would rather be with you than have all the wealth in the world. Good lady, the people who keep us apart do not realise what they are doing.

I understand, lady, that you are as much worried about me as any gentlewoman in the world. I wish God would let me take all the sadness that you have had, and that you were finished with it. For it is like death to me to hear that you are not treated the way that you should be. This is a painful life that we lead.

If you have gone against me, as I have heard that you have, you did it because you were frightened, or to please those who were around you. And if you did it for these reasons, it was a fair reason, considering the untrue stories that were told to you about me, which God knows I was never guilty of.

Though I have told them [Margery's parents] the truth, they will not believe me as much as they will believe you. So, good lady, speak plainly to them and tell the truth. And if they will not agree to it, then let it be sorted out between God, the devil and them. And I ask God that the danger that we are in will be theirs and not ours. I am depressed and sad to remember their attitude. God send them grace to make all things better. God be their guide and send them peace and rest.

Mistress I am afraid to write to you, for I understand that you have showed others the letters I wrote before. I beg you do not let any creature see this letter. As soon as you have read it, let it be burned, for I wish no man to see it.

I will not write to you again. Almighty Jesus preserve, keep and give you your heart's desire.

This letter is written with as great a pain as I ever wrote anything in my life. For in good faith I have been very sick and cannot find peace.

MARRIAGE

In the 15th century there could often be confusion about whether a person was married or not. This was because if two people promised that they wanted to marry each other then in law they were actually married. Sometimes this promise would be made in secret. This was especially likely to happen when the two people involved thought that one of their families might not agree with the marriage. This might happen if one of the people getting married was not as rich and powerful as the other. When Margery Paston promised to marry Richard Calle, the family tried to get her to take back the promise or say that she had never made it.

LETTER 5

Margaret Paston to her son Sir John Paston II.
September 1469.

I greet you well and send you God's blessing and mine. Last Thursday my mother-in-law [Agnes Paston, John Paston II's grandmother] and I were with the Bishop of Norwich and requested that he would not do anything concerning your sister [Margery Paston] until you and my brother could get together, for you have control over her as well as me. And he said plainly that he had been told so often to speak to her that he would not wait any longer and ordered me that Margery should see him the next day. And I said that I would not bring her, or send her. And he said that he would send for her himself and that she must be free to go. And he said that he well understood that her behaviour had hurt our hearts badly.

My mother and I told him that we did not believe – from what Margery had said – that she and Richard Calle were bound to each other. But that they were still free to choose.

On Friday the bishop sent for her and he spoke to her clearly and reminded her of her position in society and who were her family and friends. And that she would have more friends if she followed their advice. And if she did not, what rebuke and shame and loss she would suffer. And she said again what she had promised [to Richard Calle] and she said boldly that if these words did not make it final then she would make it quite clear before she left! These shameless words shocked me and her grandmother.

And then Calle was questioned on his own and he agreed with what she had said. I ordered my servants that she [Margery] should be banned from my house. I had given her warning and I sent a message to other people that they should not let her in.

I beg you that you do not take this too badly. For I know well that it goes to your heart and it is the same to me and to others. But remember, as I do, that all we have lost is a worthless person. For if she had been good, this would never have happened. Even if he [Calle] were to die at this very hour, I would not take her back.

Lovers in a garden. This is taken from the same romantic manuscript as the picture on page 20. Here you can see the very pointed shoes which were the height of fashion for men at the time.

LETTER 6

John Paston III to his brother Sir John Paston II.
6 May, 1476.

I understand that Mistress Fitzwalter has a sister, a virgin, wanting to marry, and that she might be given to a good man. Would you please speak to Master Fitzwalter about this matter for me? And you can tell him that I will serve him and if such a bargain can be made then both she and I will serve him and his wife and I will pay our expenses. For then he will know that I will not be leaving him.

LETTER 7

Dame Elizabeth Brews to John Paston III.
January 1476.

My husband would have you go to your mother and get hold of the £20 and then he would be happier to arrange the marriage with you. He will give you £100 and – on the day that she [Elizabeth Brews' daughter, Margery Brews] is married – my father will give her 50 marks. But if we make an agreement, I shall be giving you a great treasure; that is a clever gentlewoman, both good and virtuous. For if I were to sell her, I would not give her up for £100. But cousin, I trust you so much that I would think she was well suited to you. I would be glad that if my husband and you could agree this marriage then it might be my fortune to settle this matter. And, cousin, if this letter does not fit in with your intentions, then I ask you to burn it!

LETTER 8

Margery Brews to John Paston III.
February 1476.

To my well-loved valentine, John Paston,

I recommend myself to you longing to hear how you are. And if you are interested to hear how I am – I am not in good health either in body, or heart, nor shall I be until I hear from you!

My mother has worked hard with my father but she cannot get any more money than you know about and, God knows, I am very sorry about it. But if you love me, as I hope you do, you will not leave me. For if you had only half the wealth you have, I would not leave you!

No more to you, but the Holy Trinity look after you. And I beg you that this letter will not be seen by any creature except yourself.

CHAPTER 4

Home and Family Life

Work in the countryside. The men in the front of the picture are making a fence, while in the background men are ploughing and sowing seed. This manuscript was painted in France in the late 15th century, but similar scenes would have been very common in England.

Many of the documents in the Paston collection give information about home and family life. Not all of the documents are letters. Wills also survive (Document 1) which tell us something about how a person's possessions were divided after their death. We also learn about the great expense which followed a death in a wealthy family like the Pastons (Document 2). These costs involved things as different as making sure the body was brought home respectfully, to paying for the feast following the funeral. It was also expected that a wealthy family like the Pastons would pay for an expensive tomb for an important member of the family. It took some time to get the business sorted out (Letter 6) and they raised the money by selling expensive cloth in their possession to the King.

There were strict rules about how a family should behave following a death in the family. This behaviour was expected for some time after the funeral and it was helpful to get advice from friends about the best way to proceed (Letter 2). A death in the family could lead to a lot of changes, even to the extent of giving a relative a new job and replacing some servants (Letter 3).

Other pieces of family news are more connected with life than death. The manor house was extended, with all the upheaval that building can cause (Letter 1). Other letters are more concerned with getting a new pair of **hose** (Letter 4) or passing on general gossip (Letter 5).

DOCUMENT 1

The will of Clement Paston.
15 June, 1419

Firstly I leave my soul to Almighty God, the Blessed Mary, the Blessed Margaret and all the saints. My body is to be buried in the parish church of St Margaret at Paston, between the south door and the tomb of Beatrice, my wife.

I leave to the vicar of the church for my tithes and any other things owed to him 3 shillings and 4 pence. To the light of the Blessed Margaret in the chancel I leave 7 pounds of wax. For the repairing of the church I leave 3 shillings and 4 pence.

The rest of my belongings I leave to Margery, my sister, and to William Paston, my son, for them to pay my debts, make up for any injuries I have caused and to pay all that I owe. What is left they should spend on works of charity for my soul and the souls of Beatrice and all my ancestors.

DOCUMENT 2

A list of some of the many expenses of John Paston's funeral, 1466, including the meal after the funeral.

To 12 men carrying torches from London to Norwich:	6 pence a day.
To Martyn Savage waiting with my dead master for 7 days:	2 shillings, 10 pence.
For bread and ale for 12 men who carried the torches:	13 pence.
To the priests at the **dirge** at Bromholm [Priory]:	14 shillings.
To the glazier for taking out 2 panes of glass at the church, to let out the smell of the candles at the dirge and soldering new ones in:	20 pence.
For 27 geese:	17 shillings.
For 17 chickens:	16 shillings, 6 pence
For 22 sheep:	37 shillings, 5 pence.
For 20 gallons of milk:	20 pence.
For 4 pints of butter:	4 pence.
For 14 gallons of ale:	2 shillings.
For 13 salted fish:	4 shillings, 4 pence.

LETTER 1

Margaret Paston to her husband John Paston.
30 January, 1453.

Right worshipful husband,

I recommend myself to you and look forward to hear how you are. Sir Thomas Howes has provided four large beams for the private room and the **malthouse** and the brewery. Of these beams he has bought three. The fourth – that will be the longest and greatest – he will get from Hellesdon. He says my Master Fastolf will give it to me because my room will be made with it. As for the laying of these beams, they will be laid this next week. As for the rest, I think it can wait until you come home, because I cannot yet get hold of posts and boards.

I have measured the private room where you want your **coffers** and desk to be put for the time being. There is no space by the bed, even if the bed was moved to the door, to place both your desk and your coffers there – and still have room to sit beside them. Therefore I have arranged for you to have the same private room as you had before. And when your belongings are moved out of your little house, and your bags put in one of the great coffers they will be safe, I trust.

I ask you not to be reluctant to write letters to me between now and when you come home. If I could, I would have one every day from you! The Blessed Trinity have you in keeping. Written at Norwich, on the Tuesday after the celebration of the Conversion of St Paul.

Building a house. This is from the same French manuscript as the picture on page 27. You can see the same two men, presumably the landowner and his steward or his son, watching what is going on in both pictures. This picture shows many building techniques and tools, including the two-man saw, a windlass and pulley for lifting heavy loads, and an adze for shaping planks. Some, such as scaffolding, the wheelbarrow and the trowel, have hardly changed today.

LETTER 2

Margaret Paston to her husband John Paston.
24 December, 1459.

I sent your eldest son to my Lady Morley to find out what entertainment took place in her house the Christmas after the death of my lord, her husband. She said that there was no acting; no playing of harps, or lutes, or singing; no shameless entertainment; just the playing of board games and chess and cards. Such entertainments she gave her people permission to play.

LETTER 3

Margaret Paston to her husband John Paston.
3 December, [1461?].

My aunt has died, God forgive her soul. And if it pleases you, send a message about how you would like us to deal with her possessions. And if it would please you, have my cousin William her son join you. I know you would find him a useful man to take into your household and able to buy all kinds of things required there, and to see to the running of it. It has been told me that he has good skill in such things and, if you like, I will send for him and speak with him about it. I shall do as you instruct me, for in truth it is time to change your old servants for many reasons.

Also it is thought by my cousin, Elizabeth Clare – and the vicar and others that are your friends – that it would be useful to make friends with Hugh of Fen. For he is considered very faithful and trustworthy to his friends. And it is said that he can achieve a lot with the King and it is said that he could do a lot against those who are your enemies. And therefore, for God's sake, if you can get his goodwill don't reject it.

Also if you will be home this Christmas, it would help if you would buy pewter vessels: two basins and two jugs and twelve candlesticks. For you have too few of any of these to serve this place. The Blessed Trinity have you in his keeping.

LETTER 4

John Paston III to his mother Margaret Paston.
14 September, 1465.

After all humble and most due recommendation, as humbly as I can, I beg you for your blessing. I beg you that there may be provided some way that I might have sent home to me two pairs of hose – one pair

CLOTHING

In the 15th century most ordinary people owned far fewer clothes than people do in the 20th century. This was because their clothes were handmade and so were expensive. Richer people, of course, had more but even they paid a lot of money for them. When John Paston III ordered two new pairs of hose it cost him as much as it would have done to buy eight sheep. This was about the same amount of money as a farm labourer would have earned in a month! Most ordinary clothes were made of wool. The English woollen cloth, or textile industry was very important and many people were employed in the spinning, weaving and dyeing of woollen cloth in the Middle Ages.

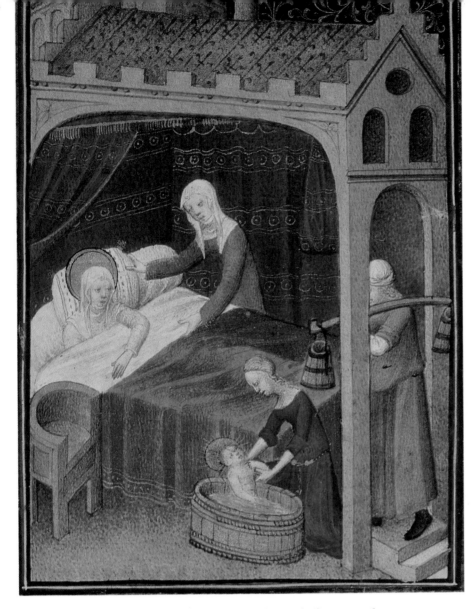

The Virgin Mary and Jesus just after the birth of Jesus, from a 15th century prayer book. It was not unusual for medieval artists to show past events as if they were happening in their own time. This picture shows the scene in a rich woman's bedroom just after she has given birth. It is shown as it would have looked at the time. There is no attempt to show the sort of clothes Mary and Jesus would have worn and they are not even in a stable.

black and another pair russet. They are ready made for me at the hosier with the crooked back – next to the Black Friar's Gate, at Ludgate [London]. John Pampynge knows him well and as the black hose are paid for, he will send me the russet pair unpaid for. I beg you that this will not be forgotten for I do not have a complete pair of hose to put on. I think that the two pairs will cost 8 shillings.

My brother [Sir John Paston II] and my sister Anne and all the garrison at Hellesdon are well, thank God, and recommend themselves to you – every one.

I ask that you visit the **Rood of Northdoor** and St Saviour, at Bermondsey, while you live in London and let my sister Margery go with you to pray to them that she may get a good husband before she goes home again. Written at Norwich, Holy Cross day.

LETTER 5

Sir John Paston II to his brother John Paston III.
3 February, 1473.

As for the news here there is only a little, except that the Duke of Burgundy is well and my lady, his wife, is well. I was with them last Thursday at Ghent. Peter Metteney is well as is Mrs Gretkin and Rabeky asks to be remembered to you. She has been ill but it has done her good and she looks better and slimmer now than she was. And whenever she was cheerful, would ask me saucily – 'How is your brother Master John?' I was angry at this and jealous that she should care so much for you, when I was there!

Send me word of how my lord and lady and all the court think of me. I hear also that my lady, and yours, Dame Margaret Vere is dead – God have her soul. If I am not sorry to hear it, I know that you will be.

No more to you at this time but Almighty God have you in his keeping. Written at Calais the 3rd day of February, in the 12th year of the reign of Edward IV.

LETTER 6

Sir John Paston II to his mother Margaret Paston.
13 May, 1478.

To my right worshipful mother,

I intend to be at home this Midsummer and intend, with your good help, to begin work on my father's tomb so that the work will be completed this summer.

Be pleased to know that I spoke with Master Pykenham to know if he would buy the gold cloth for the price he once wanted to pay for it. He once offered me 20 marks for it, although it cost me £24. Yet now when I spoke to him about it, he refused to buy it.

But the King is having made **copes** and **vestments,** which he intends to give to the college at Fotheringhay, where my lord, his father, is now buried and he pays a good price! I asked the vestment maker to buy twelve yards. If it pleases you the sale of the cloth will be used to pay for a tomb for my father at Bromholm. I promise that by Michaelmas there shall be a tomb over my father's grave. There shall be none like it in Norfolk. And God send me leisure so that I may come home; if I do not, the money will not be put to any other use, but it will be kept by someone you trust until it may be used in the way that I have written. Otherwise I will have given you cause never to trust me, while you and I live.

To be thought of as really important in 15th century England people needed to own a lot of land. The people who owned the greatest amounts of land were called the 'nobles', or 'nobility'. Amongst the nobles there was often great rivalry. A noble who made mistakes and fell from power could lose his life (Letter 1). The Duke of Suffolk signed a peace treaty with the French which was very unpopular. Enemies at court had him murdered.

During the 15th century the Paston family's wealth and importance increased. They realised that the most powerful people in the country were those who daily served the King. This group of people was known as the court.

In the court – which moved about the country – there was the chance that a loyal and intelligent person would be 'noticed' and rewarded (Letter 2). There was also the chance that a person could make powerful friends who would offer help and protection. These powerful 'patrons' could have a great effect on a person's plans. The Pastons were involved in so many arguments over land and property that powerful friends were very valuable indeed to them. The Pastons made great efforts to be noticed at court, despite problems (Letter 4). They were much interested in court life (Letter 7, from a good friend).

CHAPTER 5

Court and Nobility

The Tournament of St Anglevert, 1390. Notice the barrier which kept the horses apart during jousting.

Earl Rivers gives a book to Edward IV, from a manuscript book made in the 1470s. This sort of manuscript book is the type from which most of the pictures in this book are taken. Within ten years of this mansucript being made the first printed books in England were produced.

LETTER 1

William Lomner to John Paston.
5 May, 1450.

Right worshipful sir,

I recommend myself to you and must say I am very sorry about what I must say and have washed this little letter with sorrowful tears.

On the Monday after Mayday news came to London that on the previous Thursday the Duke of Suffolk arrived at the coast of Kent, near Dover, with his two ships and a little **pinnace**. This pinnace he sent with certain letters to certain of his trusted men in Calais to find out how he would be welcomed. And he was met by a ship called *Nicholas of the Tower*, along with other ships. The captain of the

Nicholas discovered from those who were in the pinnace that the duke was coming. And when he saw the duke's ships, he sent out a boat to find out who they were. And the duke himself spoke to them and said that by the King's command he was going to Calais.

And they said he must speak to their master. And so with two or three of his men, he went with them on their boat to the *Nicholas*. And when he arrived, the master said to him 'Welcome traitor!' And then the master wanted to know if the men on the ships would stand by the duke and they sent word that they would not! And so the duke was in the *Nicholas* until the next Saturday.

Some say that he wrote many things to be sent to the King, but that is not really known. And some say that he was tried on the ship on the charges against him and found guilty.

And in the sight of all the men he was taken from the great ship in a boat. And there was an axe and a block and one of the most shameless on the ship told him to lay down his head and he would be treated fairly and die on a sword. And he took a rusty sword and cut off his head with half a dozen cuts and took away his russet coloured gown and his doublet of mailed velvet and laid his body on the sands of Dover. And some say his head was set on a pole by it.

LETTER 2

*Margaret Paston to her husband John Paston.
20 April, 1453.*

Right worshipful husband,

I recommend myself to you. As for news, the Queen came into this town on Tuesday last, after noon, and stayed there until it was Thursday, at three after noon. And she sent for my cousin, Elizabeth Clere, to come to her and she did not dare to disobey her command and came to her. And when she came into the Queen's presence, the Queen made much of her and desired her to have a husband. But despite this, a husband is as far away as ever!

The Queen was very pleased with her reply and spoke of her well and said that, since she came into Norfolk, she had seen no gentlewoman that she liked better.

The **bailiff** of Swaffham was here with the King's brother [either Henry VI's half-brother Edmund Tudor, or Jasper Tudor] and he came to me, thinking that you were at home, and said that the King's brother desired that he would ask you to come to him. And he told me that he would send for you when he comes to London.

THE ROYAL COURT
The royal court was made up of the people who served the King and the Queen. This included everyone from the people who cooked and served the meals to the rich and important people who looked after the money and gave the King and Queen advice. The King and Queen often travelled around the countryside. This was a way of keeping control of the country and made sure that they were seen and known. The rich and ambitious people in the country were very keen to be noticed by the King or Queen. This might give them a very powerful friend who would provide them with jobs and help them in arguments with other powerful people.

LETTER 3

Edmund Clere to John Paston.
9 January, 1455.

Right beloved cousin,

Blessed be God, the King is well and has been since Christmas. On Saint John's day he commanded his **almoner** to ride to Canterbury with his offering.

And on the Monday afternoon the Queen came to him and brought my lord prince with her. And then the King asked what the prince's name was and the Queen told him 'Edward' And then the King held up his hands and thanked God. And he said that up until that time he never knew, or understood, what was said to him, or where he had been, while he was sick. And he asked who were the godfathers and the Queen told him and he was well pleased.

And my Lord of Winchester and my Lord [the Prior] of St John's were with him on the day after **Twelfthday** and he spoke to them as well as he had ever done. And when they came out they wept for joy.

And he says he is full of love for all the world. And now he says **matins** of Our Lady and **evensong** and hears his mass devoutly.

Written at Greenwich, on Thursday after Twelfthday.

LETTER 4

Clement Paston to his brother John Paston.
25 August, 1461.

Right reverend and worshipful brother,

I feel that my nephew [John Paston III] has few friends in the King's house. And the officials of the King's house do not yet treat him as part of it. For the cooks have not been ordered to serve him! The **sewer** will not give him any dishes, for the sewer will not take any man dishes, until commanded by the King's controller. Also, the only person he knows is John Wykes. And Wykes has told him that he will bring him to meet the King, but he has not yet done so.

As a result it is best for him to take his leave and come home, until you have spoken with someone to help him, for he is not bold enough to put himself forward. But then I wonder that if he should come home,

the King would find that when he needed him, you would have him at home which would stop him being regarded with favour. Also, men would think he had been sacked from serving the King!

Also Pekok [a friend] tells me that his money is spent – not riotously but wisely and carefully; for it costs more to be in the King's household, when he is travelling, than you thought it would be. And therefore we must get him 100 shillings at least and even that will be too little. I shall have to lend it to him from my own silver. If I definitely knew your intention was that he should come home I would not send him any. But I will do what I think will please you best and that, I think, is to send him the silver. Therefore, I ask you as quickly as you can, send me 5 marks and the rest, I believe, I shall get from Christopher Hanson and Luket [other friends]. I ask you to send it to me as quickly as you can, for I shall leave myself quite bare! Send me a letter telling how you would want him treated.

Written on Tuesday after St Bartholomew's day. Christ protect you.

Fortune with her wheel, from a 15th century manuscript. The picture of Fortune, or chance, as a spinning wheel which would leave you sometimes up and sometimes down was widespread at the time. It is not only found in painting, but also in the poetry of Chaucer and other writers.

A lady and her knight, from a 15th century romance similar to the one from which the pictures on pages 20 and 25 have been taken.

LETTER 5

John Paston III to his mother Margaret Paston.
8 July, 1468.

My lord, the Bastard [the Count of de la Roche, called the Bastard of Burgundy] answered the challenge to **joust** of 24 knights within eight days, at **jousts of peace**. And when they had fought, these knights and himself would **tourney** with another 25 the next day, which is next Monday. And those who have jousted with him have been as richly dressed as him, in cloth of gold and silk and silver. For of such gear and gold and pearls and precious stones the people of the duke's court have as much as they want.

And as for the duke's court – the lords, ladies, gentlewomen, knights, esquires and gentlemen – I never heard of anything like it, except King Arthur's court. And in truth, I have not the skill, or memory, to write to you about half the excellence that is here. But, as I remember it, I will tell you when I come home, which I trust to God will not be long.

LETTER 6

Sir John Paston II to his brother John Paston III.
3 June, 1473.

Right worshipful brother,

I am now poorly supplied [with men] which is likely to keep me here this Whitsuntide [Whitsunday, 6 June, 1473]. Therefore if you know any likely men – good archers – send them to me and I will have them and they shall have four marks a year and my **livery**.

I ask you, send me a new vestment of white **damask**, which is amongst my other gear at Norwich. I will make an **arming doublet** of it – though next time I would give a long gown of velvet for another vestment – and send it quickly to me.

I hope to be very merry at Calais, this Whitsuntide and I am well dressed and furnished.

LETTER 7

William Makefire to his Masters Roger Darsy and Gulis Alyngton.
17 January, 1506.

Right worshipful masters,

I recommend myself to you, letting you know that the King's grace [Henry VII of England] and the King of Castile [King Philip] met this day at three o'clock, two miles out of Windsor, and there the King received him in the best manner that I ever saw and each of them embraced the other in his arms.

To show you what the King of England wore, this is what it was: his **bay** horse was **trapped** with needlework, a gown of purple velvet, a chain with a **gorge** of diamonds and a hood of purple velvet. And the King of Castile rode on a **sorrel hobby-horse**, which the King gave to him. His clothing was all black – a gown of black velvet, a black hood, a black hat and his horse's harness of black velvet.

When the King rode forth to Windsor Castle he rode on the right hand of the King of Castile. And when they dismounted, the King of Castile was off his horse a good space before our King was dismounted. And then the King's grace offered to take him by the arm, which he would not do, but took the King by his arm. And so they went to the King of Castile's room, which is the richest decorated that I ever saw: seven chambers together, hung with cloth from Arras, made with gold as thick as could be. And as for three beds of state, no other Christian king could show such as these.

TOURNAMENTS

Tournaments were a very dangerous and popular sport. They involved knights fighting each other in public in armour. They trained knights to fight and through them some knights became famous and sometimes very rich. Tournaments became popular in the 12th century and were still going on in the 16th century. Many mock battles were fought at a tournament. A 'joust' was fought between two knights on horses. Often they included fights between groups of people called a mélée. There was often fighting between two knights on foot. Knights captured lost their armour and often had to pay money before they could be set free.

CHAPTER 6

Sickness and Health

To the people of the late Middle Ages, sickness and death were a familiar part of life. Diseases and infections were common and ways of treating illnesses were often unable to make the sick person better. This was particularly so when the disease affected a person's mind (Letter 9).

The letters show that one of the popular medicines within the family was 'treacle of Genoa'. Treacle, or syrup, it was hoped, would remove infections from the body. In the letters the requests for treacle, or syrup, occur a number of times (Letters 1, 2, 4 and 7). The family were keen to make sure that the medicine was pure and that it had not been opened (Letter 2 again).

There is also a request that a plaster, or poultice, should be sent to ease the pain of an injured knee, along with instructions about how it should be used (Letter 8).

During the 15th century a number of **epidemics** occurred. Epidemic diseases swept through the country, killing a large number of people. It is not always easy for a modern historian to tell what the disease actually was but such epidemics were well known in Norwich (Letter 7 again) and led people to try and escape from the city, although the disease was clearly all over the country (Letter 5). Already people were beginning to see a connection between dirt and disease (Letter 6) and distrusted the skills of those who 'claimed' that they could cure the illnesses (Letter 3).

LETTER 1

Margaret Paston to her husband John Paston.
1 July, 1451.

I was at dinner on St Peter's day. There my Lady Felbrygg and some other gentlewomen wished you could have been there. They said they would all have been the happier if you had been there. I ask you heartily that you will quickly send me a pot of treacle. For I have been very worried, and your daughter too, since you rode away. One of the tallest young men in this parish lies sick and has a great fever. What will happen to him, God knows. I have sent my Uncle Berney the pot of treacle that you had bought for him.

Sir Henry Inglose has passed to God this night, whose soul God forgive. He was carried forth today at 9 o'clock to St Faith's Priory, and there he shall be buried. If you want to buy any of his stuff, I ask you to send me word about it quickly. The Blessed Trinity have you in his keeping. Written at Norwich, on the Thursday after St Peter's day.

LETTER 2

John Paston II to his mother Margaret Paston.
Exact date unknown, but between 1460 and 1470.

Be pleased to know that I am sending you three treacle pots. My **apothecary** swears to me they were never undone and of these you can have as many as you want. Nevertheless my brother, John, sent to me for two. Therefore, I ask you that he may have at least one. There is one pot which is marked under the bottom two times, with the letters 'M.P.'

This pot I trust the most. And after this pot, the twisted pot. And I distrust the pot which has the piece chipped off the most, because it might have been undone. Also, the other two pots are printed with the maker's mark two times on the covering, but the other pot is only marked once. Despite this, I had the same promise for all of them that they had not been opened.

A woman preparing medicine, from a manuscript painted in 1470. Although not allowed to be doctors women played an important part in medicine. In rich families women often treated people, instead of doctors. Amongst the poor the local wise woman usually offered the only treatment available.

LETTER 3

Margaret Paston to her husband John Paston.
8 June 1464.

It is said that the Duke of Suffolk has come home and either he is dead or else very sick and not likely to survive. For God's sake beware of any medicine that you get from any **physicians** in London. I shall never trust them because of what happened to your father and my uncle, whose souls God forgive.

LETTER 4

Margaret Paston to her husband John Paston.
5 February, 1470.

I greet you well and send you God's blessing and mine. I send you by the carrier of this and enclosed in this letter, five gold shillings and ask you to buy me a **sugarloaf** and dates and almonds and send them home to me. And if it costs any more money I will pay you again when you come home. The Holy Ghost keep you and deliver you from your enemies. Written on St Agnes' day in a hurry.

Also, I ask you to speak to Master Roger for my syrup. For I have never needed it more. And send it to me as quickly as you can.

LETTER 5

Sir John Paston II to his brother John Paston III.
15 September, 1471.

I ask you send me word if any of our friends or well-wishers are dead, for I fear that there is great death in Norwich and in other towns in Norfolk. I assure you that it is the most widespread death [plague] that there ever was in England. For, in truth, I have not heard – from pilgrims who travel the country and men who ride through the country – that any **borough** town in England is free from the sickness. For God's sake, let my mother take care of my younger family, that they are not in any place where the sickness is reigning. Nor should they meet with any young people who go where the sickness is. And if any have died of that sickness in Norwich, for God's sake let her send them to some friends of hers in the country. And you follow my advice too.

Monks praying over a coffin from an early 15th century manuscript book.
For about 100 years after the Black Death first devastated Europe in the
late 1340s, death became a favourite topic for artists.

PLAGUE

There were many dreadful infectious diseases in the 15th century which were referred to at the time as 'plague', or 'pestilence'. Some of these were outbreaks of Bubonic Plague. This had first appeared in England in 1348 and was a terrible disease until it died out at the end of the 17th century. However, there were many other diseases which caused the deaths of many thousands of people. These included smallpox, measles and typhoid. Many of these diseases came from the lack of clean conditions and continued to kill people because no one understood what caused them or how they could be cured. Some of the dirtiest conditions were found in towns and there were often outbreaks of disease there. Richer people would often try to escape to their houses in the country to get away from the danger.

LETTER 6

Sir John Paston II to his mother Margaret Paston.
29 October 1479.

Be pleased to know that I have been here in London a fortnight. The first four days I was in such fear of the sickness, and also found my chamber and stuff not as clean as I expected, which worried me a lot. As I told you when I left, I did not have much money, for I had little more than 10 marks. Therefore, I beg you, to send me 100 shillings. This matter has troubled me so that it has made me half sick, as God help me.

LETTER 7

John Paston III to his brother Sir John Paston II.
6 November, 1479.

Sir, I ask you to send me, with the next man who comes from London, two pots of treacle from Genoa. They will cost 16 pence for I have used that which I had on my young wife and my young people and myself. And I shall pay the person who brings it to me. I ask you to do it quickly. Many people are dying in Norwich and especially around my house. But my wife and my women do not go out and we cannot get further away, for since I left Swainsthorpe, many people have died and been sick in every house in the town.

LETTER 8

John Paston III to his wife Margery Paston.
Undated but between 1487 and 1495.

Mistress Margery,

I recommend myself to you and send me as quickly as possible, by the next reliable messenger that you can get, a large plaster [or poultice] for the king's **attorney**, James Hobart. For although his disease is only an ache in the knees, he is the man who brought you and me together. And I would rather that your plaster stopped his pain, than have 40 shillings!

But when you send me the plaster you must write to me telling me how it should be put on and taken off the knee. And how long it should stay on the knee. And how long the plaster will be of any use and whether, or not, he must wrap any cloth around the plaster to keep it warm. And God be with you.

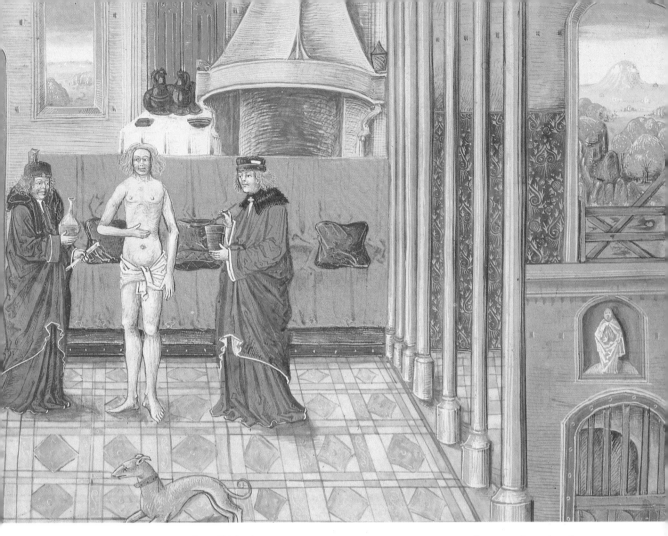

LETTER 9

The Earl of Oxford to John Paston III.
26 June, 1503.

Right worshipful and beloved,

I commend myself heartily to you. Because your brother, William, my servant, is so unwell with sickness and crazed in his mind, I cannot keep him with me. I am very sorry about this. I am sending him to you, asking that he may be tenderly looked after with you, until God wills him to be better and his mind is more peaceful.

Two doctors and a patient from a late 15th century manuscript book. This book was written 200 years before and was one of the most copied manuscripts in the Middle Ages. This section tells doctors about diseases and how they should be treated.

Glossary

alderman a person with responsibility for running a town.

almoner a person who gives out money to good causes.

apothecary a person who makes and sells medicines.

arming doublet jacket worn under armour.

Ascension of Our Lord the occasion of the ascent of Jesus Christ to Heaven 40 days after his Resurrection – a holy day in the Christian Church calendar.

assize county law court visited periodically by the royal justices.

attorney a lawyer.

bailiff a person responsible for running a manor.

bay chesnut colour, often used to describe a horse.

bill a letter, or document.

borough a town with power to run some of its own affairs.

brigander a type of body armour.

Candlemas a Church holy day remembering the presentation of Christ in the temple on 2 February.

Captain of Calais commander of the English soldiers at the town of Calais in France.

chamber a room, usually private.

Chancellor high ranking official, in charge of the King's government.

coffer a wooden chest.

constable a person with the job of keeping law and order.

Constable of England high ranking member of the King's government.

cope long cloak worn by a priest during a service.

council group of important people who gave advice to the King.

court the large group of people who served the King and looked after his needs.

cuirasses armour – the breast plate and back plate.

damask silk or linen material.

dirge song sung at funeral service.

doublet man's clothing, like a tight fitting jacket.

ducat a coin of gold, or silver.

epidemic rapidly spreading disease which takes hold in a community at a particular time.

esquire the rank below that of knight.

evensong the church service held just before sunset.

extortion forcing something, often money, from someone.

frese type of cloth.

friars a religious order or brotherhood of men who devoted their lives to God.

garrison a group of soldiers defending a town, or castle.

gorge a piece of amour worn at the throat.

hobby a small horse.

hose clothing worn by men, like thick tights.

Hundred Court a law court dealing with a local area.

jacks a type of body armour.

jousts mock fights between knights on horseback.

joust of peace a joust fought with blunted weapons designed to avoid serious injuries.

justices royal judges who travelled the country sitting in the county assize courts.

livery clothes or uniform worn by all the servants and soldiers of a wealthy household to show whose men they were.

malthouse A place for treating grain as part of the making of alcohol.

manor land, often with a house and buildings, owned by a wealthy person.

mark sum of money worth 13 shillings and 4 pence. Over a month's pay for a 15th century farm labourer.

mass   the Christian Church service of Holy Communion.

matins   the Church service held before the mass on Sunday – early morning.

Michaelmas   the feast of St Michael [September 29].

Middle Ages   period of history once thought of as lasting from about AD1066–1485 but now often thought of as having started with the collapse of the Roman Empire.

noble   a gold coin, also called a 'Royal'. Worth 10 **shillings**. About a month's pay for a 15th century farm labourer.

Our Lady of Walsingham   the church of the Virgin Mary at Walsingham, visited by many pilgrims.

oversail   overtake

penny/pence   a silver coin which was used in everyday buying and selling. There were 240 in a pound [£]. About the price of a gallon of milk in the 15th century.

physician   a doctor.

pinnace   a small sailing boat which accompanied a warship as messenger or scout.

privy seal   official stamp on wax, used on documents which did not need the Great Seal. Held by a high ranking member of the royal government.

quarrels   crossbow bolts; a kind of arrow.

Rood of Northdoor   a place of worship in London, thought to be holy.

sallets   type of helmet.

score   twenty

seal   a stamp made on hot wax to show a document is official and used to close it.

service   work which a tenant owed to the lord.

sewer   person who is in charge of servants bringing food to the table in a wealthy household.

sheriff   person representing the ruler in each shire.

shilling   a sum of money. There were 20 shillings in a pound [£]. About the price of a sheep in the 15th century.

shire   an area of local government; a county [eg. Wiltshire, Yorkshire].

shireday   meeting of representatives of people in a shire to enforce the law and receive royal commands.

siege   to surround a castle, or town, in an attempt to capture it.

skirmish   unplanned fight between small parties.

sorrel   a reddish-brown colour. Often used to describe a horse.

sugarloaf   a large and expensive lump of sugar.

tenants   people who rent land on a manor.

tithe   a tax paid to the church.

tourney   a mock battle, usually involving a group of knights.

Treasurer   high ranking official who looked after the royal money.

trapped   word used to describe a horse clothed with flowing material.

Trinity   in Christianity, the Father, Son and Holy Ghost as constituting one God.

Tudors   family who became rulers of England in 1485.

twelfthday/night   celebration, twelve days after Christmas.

vestments   official garments of the clergy worn during church services.

vestry   part of a church where the priest changed into his vestments.

ward   a district of a town under the jurisdiction of an alderman.

Wars of the Roses   series of wars fought in England in the 15th century.

Whitsunday   festival of the church on the 7th Sunday after Easter, remembering the descent of the Holy Spirit upon the Apostles.

wykets   holes in a building, to fire guns out of.

wyndlacs   a hook used to wind up a crossbow ready for firing.

Index

Numbers in *italic* type refer to illustrations; numbers in **bold** type refer to information boxes.